I0036951

STEWARDSHIP GOD'S WAY GUIDEBOOK

KENDALL DAVIS

Reliquia PUBLISHING

CHERISHING STORIES FOR A LIFETIME

CONTENTS

HOW TO USE THIS GUIDEBOOK

The Stewardship God's Way Guidebook is a supplementary resource that further expands on the lessons presented in the Stewardship God's Way book. It is a companion text designed to reemphasize and reflect on the practical applications found within the book "Stewardship God's Way," helping you apply its teachings to your daily life. We hope that by organizing and applying, you will gain insight into your financial situation and improve your future for the glory of the Lord. By the time you complete the guidebook, you will have a clear picture of where you can make improvements to reach your stewardship goals. You can make copies of the forms for future use, but I kindly insist that you refrain from copying the guidebook for distribution. Not only is it copyrighted, but purchasing it is part of a participant's stewardship process.

This guidebook is a personal and small-group guide to biblical stewardship. Start by scanning the QR code and watching a short video for your encouragement. The focus is not only filling in the blank lines on the page, but on filling the blank spaces in our hearts that hinder us from being responsible stewards. Our prayer is that in handling your finances with obedience and excellence, your intimacy with Jesus Christ grows richer, that you would be a light in Christ's church, and that you would live life in full abundance.

To Group Facilitators: We ask that you study to show yourself approved. Explore each topic in greater depth. You are not just helping finances; you are helping families and futures. There are biblical lessons for individual and small group learning. There are three parts to each section: Approach, Assess & Apply. We approach the concepts in review, assess what scripture speaks about the topic and its relevance to us today, and apply its principles of stewardship to our lives.

KINGDOM STEWARDSHIP

A PICTURE OF THE KING'S STEWARD

Watch the short video: Spiritual Capital

Read Chapter 1 and Find the Word

B	I	P	M	A	N	A	G	E	R	H	O	E	Y	X	J	V	K
D	G	I	O	W	N	E	R	S	W	D	C	T	R	K	B	D	X
N	H	H	S	B	Z	N	I	X	B	N	I	Z	D	C	O	S	Q
I	B	S	L	O	P	C	T	K	E	L	R	F	L	O	L	K	X
F	L	D	O	C	I	T	N	U	I	K	D	W	I	W	G	E	J
F	E	R	Y	I	Q	I	L	B	S	E	X	E	W	E	P	N	T
Q	I	A	A	Q	N	F	A	I	G	E	N	E	R	O	U	S	K
G	W	W	L	C	N	T	O	O	L	C	K	J	G	R	V	T	F
U	X	E	B	I	N	G	B	M	M	A	G	L	V	O	G	Z	C
W	E	T	Y	U	C	E	N	R	L	R	O	R	G	N	O	A	P
F	O	S	O	I	S	H	Y	N	E	W	E	N	I	A	Z	A	G
N	B	C	E	E	B	L	F	E	Q	T	Q	D	T	N	R	V	Z
F	C	D	P	J	R	V	D	P	S	R	R	W	B	T	X	J	H
A	Z	A	B	V	O	V	L	A	F	A	I	T	H	F	U	L	C
F	I	T	M	M	O	H	M	Q	O	O	C	K	B	R	L	S	A
X	J	M	X	D	H	H	U	H	R	B	X	F	T	F	R	C	W
P	U	V	S	N	L	P	U	B	P	Z	L	Y	O	C	M	L	H
G	N	M	T	B	S	Y	J	K	E	Q	O	R	G	R	S	V	P

Accountability	Fox	Trap
Influence	God	Greed
Stewardship	Tool	Master
Faithful	Generous	Hoarding
Loyal	Manager	Owner

LEANING IMPLICATIONS:

How alert are you to your responsibility and the implications of your stewardship? There are daily attacks on believers' financial security, attempting to persuade us to do what is easiest rather than what is right. Are you ready to stand on God's word?

ASSESS

A PICTURE OF THE KING'S STEWARD

We are not owners but **stewards** of everything we have

"As each has received a gift, employ it in serving one another,
as good managers of the grace of God in its various forms"
1 Peter 4:10

Requirements of a Steward

- The Steward is _____ (1 Corinthians 4:2)

- The Steward is _____ (Colossians 3:23-24)

- The Steward is _____ (Proverbs 11:25)

The Steward's Enemy

- The Bible calls Satan _____ (2 Corinthians 4:4).

  What does this mean? _____

  _____

  _____

  _____

  _____

What can Satan offer _____ (Matthew 4:8-9)

Why would you turn this down? _____

_____

_____

_____

- Who is our second Enemy? _____ (1 John 2:15)

  How can you overcome this? _____

  _____

  _____

  _____

(John 16:33, 1 John 5:4, James 4:4, Romans 12:2, Revelation 12:11)

- Who is our most significant Enemy? _____ (Romans 8:7-8)

- How do we overcome this? _____

  _____

  _____

  _____

(1 Corinthians 6:18, 2 Corinthians 10:5, Colossians 3:5, Galatians 5:16-18)

A Steward should not:

- _____ (Proverbs 15:27)

- _____ (1 Timothy 6:10)

- _____ (Proverbs 23:4)

- _____ (Psalms 101:7)

- _____ (Proverbs 23:6-7)

Your net worth to the world is usually determined by what remains
after your bad habits are subtracted from your good ones.
~ Benjamin Franklin.

Titles we call a Steward

Managers	As managers, stewards follow the wishes of others. We manage affairs on behalf of God following His plans.
Supervisors	The steward oversees a task to ensure compliance, cooperation, and completion. They make sure everything is in its proper place.
Caretaker	Caretaking speaks to the heart of love that a steward is to show in all their task. They perform a labor of love in the name of the Lord.
Trustee	Stewardship is a trust and takes faith and faithfulness. God entrusts us with the task that he created us with the ability to complete
Administrator	Ministry is service, and administration is the act of enhancing service in innovative ways that improve the workplace.
Guardian	Stewards are protectors. They witness, watch, and warn of trouble, standing in the gap with God against the harm of infiltration.

APPLY

Prayer: Father, help me to know who I am as your steward. I desire to follow your plan faithfully. Please help me to discern when I have slipped and grant me the wisdom to make the proper corrections. I ask that your Holy Spirit guide me into all truth and righteousness so that I can be a light to this world. I take responsibility for managing the affairs of my home, realizing you are the head of the Christian life. Grant me strength, tenacity, and favor as I do my task, for your kingdom's purpose. Guard my family and life as I serve where you call me, in the matchless name of Jesus Christ, Amen.

NOTES:

_____

_____

_____

_____

_____

_____

_____

_____

_____

_____

_____

_____

_____

_____

_____

_____

_____

_____

_____

_____

_____

_____

_____

NET WORTH WORKSHEET

ASSETS

Checking and Savings accounts . . . . $ _____

Principal Home and Rental Properties . . . . $ _____

Vehicles and boats value . . . . $ _____

Furniture and equipment value . . . . $ _____

Money market account, savings bonds, and CDs . . . . $ _____

Investment and Retirement Accounts . . . . $ _____

IRA, Roth IRA, 401(k) and Pension . . . . $ _____

Brokerage Accounts . . . . $ _____

Business Ownership Interest . . . . $ _____

Other . . . . $ _____

Total Assets $ _____

LIABILITIES

Mortgage and property loan balances . . . . $ _____

Credit card balance . . . . $ _____

Student and Vehicle loans balance . . . . $ _____

Medical Bills . . . . $ _____

Income tax owed . . . . $ _____

Other . . . . $ _____

Total Liabilities $ _____

NET WORTH = TOTAL ASSETS - TOTAL LIABILITIES $ _____

THE LEGACY JOURNEY

GUIDE SECTION TWO

THE STEWARDS LEGACY

Watch the short video: Generational Success

THE STEWARDS LEGACY

HITTING THE RIGHT TARGET

A good steward has targeted insight. Targeted insight is a operational objective that understands how to best apply what you need to have in hand to see and achieve an desired affect. God **GAVE (Goals, Assignment, Vision, Equipment)** us what we need to hit the targets He set before us.

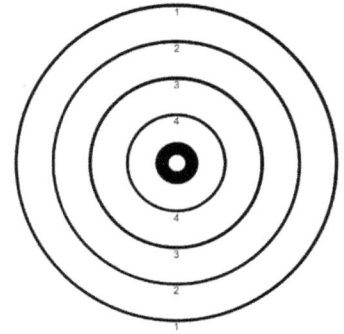

Goals: GOAL (Goal, Objective, Activities, Lessons); Goals and objectives go hand in hand, but differ in that an objective is a desired outcome, and goals are how you achieve your objectives. Goals are the means to reaching an end that we established to hit the target we call objectives. Our activity is what takes us to the goal, and the lessons we learn help us adjust to ensure we have the right goals.

Assignment: An assignment is a task that God gives us to do. It is our mission or the lane we are to stay in. It is knowing you are doing the right thing in your life. Mission is a God given assignment to fulfill His plan for your life. Our mission or assignment is what we are to do, and purpose is the reason why we do it.

Vision: A vision is a hopeful and expected outcome that God has revealed to individuals regarding their personal lives. Vision always includes your values, which are things we hold as valuable, virtuous, and victorious. Without vision, we can't see the target and may hit the wrong thing.

Equipment: Being equipped means that we have the proper TAGS (Tools, Abilities, Gifts, Skills) to complete the job. It causes us to acquire resources, increase knowledge, and develop our abilities. Before taking any action, we must ensure that we are adequately equipped to achieve our objectives.

Chapter 2 of the book presents four methods by which money can be both legally and morally earned. They are the PIES of earning. A wise steward seeks to earn money from any legitimate source that won't compromise what **PAVES (Purpose, Authority, Values, Ethics, Spirit)** their way. List the ways you participate or potentially could participate in **PIES (Products, Investments, Eligibilities, Services).**

Products: What could you make or purchase at a low price for reselling?

_____

_____

_____

_____

Investments: Do you know where your investments stand and how they work?

_____

_____

_____

Eligibilities: Are there any benefits or programs that you can use that you haven't applied for?

_____

_____

_____

Services: What services can you provide that can be useful, earning you extra Income or helping in ministry work?

_____

_____

_____

CREATING A LEGACY

Christian success is not like worldly success, which is measured by money and possessions to please others. Our success is a mission and purpose to please God.

"For am I now seeking the favor of men, or of God? Or am I striving to please men? For if I were still pleasing men, I wouldn't be a servant of Christ."
Galatians 1:10

Legacy Making Goals Are:

- Plans to _____ (Jeremiah 29:11)

- Require _____ (Philippians 4:13)

- Depend on _____ (Proverbs 16:3)

- Need _____ (1 Corinthians 4:2)

A Legacy of Success Comes From the ARROW:

Accountability (Galatians 6:4): How accountable are you in your actions, and who are your mentor(s) and accountability partners?

_____

_____

_____

_____

Readiness (Ecclesiastes 10:10): What have you done to get ready for opportunities, and what still needs to be done?

_____

_____

_____

Restraint (Proverbs 10:4): What have you given up to accomplish your goals and gain balance in your life and actions? What still needs to be done?

_____

_____

_____

_____

Opportunity (Revelations 3:8): In what ways have you positioned yourself for open doors? Is there anything else you need to do or give up?

_____

_____

_____

Willingness (Psalms 20:4): Describe what you are passionate about and what you believe you can achieve that will help build your financial future.

_____

_____

_____

PLACING SUCCESS UNDER THE GUN

"And Jesus increased in wisdom and stature, and in favor with God and men."
Luke 2:52

The stewards should not remain stagnant but see to grow regardless of age or station in life. Increasing in wisdom requires us to learn and grow. Increased stature comes from putting in the work that will grow us, and increasing in favor means we have to nurture relationships. Chapter 2 of the book describes each portion of the **GUN (Growth, Understanding, Nurturing)** work ethic. List what commitments you will make to achieve this:

Growth

If you say you work hard, do you truly believe it, or are there areas where you can improve? What commitment will you make to show up more for yourself and work on your own vision so you aren't just working on someone else's?

_____

_____

_____

_____

Understanding

What commitment will you make to know more about your area of business than anyone else? Can you commit to the learning plan in the book? If not, write out a plan you will stick to.

_____

_____

_____

_____

Nurturing

Relationships need to be nurtured, and to do so, you must intentionally carve out time to focus on them. What is your daily devotion plan for time with God and your family?

_____

_____

_____

_____

WRITING THE VISION (HABAKKUK 2:2-3)

Write a vision statement for the business, side hustle, or ministry that you believe the Lord has you leaning towards. Make it short and simple.

_____

_____

_____

List 3 Goals that will help you achieve the vision statement.

1. _____

2. _____

3. _____

NOTES:

_____

_____

_____

_____

_____

_____

_____

_____

_____

_____

_____

_____

SERVICE OVER SENTIMENT

GUIDE SECTION THREE

SMART SERVICE

Watch the short video: Priorities Lead to Perserverence

SMART SERVICE

STRATEGY OVER SENTIMENT

Stewardship is a rational enterprise, not an emotional struggle. Sentiment is a motivating factor that causes us to desire to help relieve suffering. Strategy is a blueprint for efficient accomplishment. The steward does not put a lid on their sentiment; they place a filter so they can do more with less. Sentiment will have you helping one person using enough to help four. It is not only wasteful but also opens us up to manipulation, which a solid strategy would prevent.

> *"Listen to counsel and receive instruction, that you may be wise in your latter end.*
> *Listen to counsel and receive instruction, that you may be wise in your latter end."*
> *Proverbs 19:20*

COMMON DECENCY VS. COMMON SENSE

Strategy over sentiment is a struggle between the common decency to help those in need and the common sense to determine the most effective way to help. Sentiment often causes you to give what you have so you can avoid regret if you ignore the person in need, but once given, the individual feels good and tends to forget about their future needs. In both cases, we forget the person in need, but at different times. Sentiment without strategy is an open door for spiritual warfare, allowing the Enemy in as you discover someone has taken advantage of your kindness. Strategy maintains sentiment but uses a plan to meet needs. Strategy doesn't forget need; it plans for it. It appears to do more than one could with a one-time moment of giving.

Sentiment	Strategy
$10 can provide a homeless person with a meal, so they will not go to sleep hungry. But the next day, they are in the same spot.	$10 given to an organization like Feeding America or No Hungry Kid provides one hundred hot meals (Yes, 100)
Standing on a corner with pictures of someone who died and needs help covering the funeral costs may have you emptying your pockets.	Morticians ask you to obtain the individual's name and the name of the funeral home they are at, as paying directly avoids scams.
Crowdfunding is an effective online tool to raise funds for those with an immediate need. People with sentiment will ask you to pitch in	Make sure those asking you to give know the individuals personally. There is a suspected 60% uptick in crowdsourcing scams.

TWO UNJUST STEWARDS

John 12:3-8 portrays Judas as an unjust steward who, within that week, would be removed from his position. Compare Judas with the unjust steward in Luke 16:1-13. What similarities can you find between Judas and the other unjust steward?

_____

_____

_____

_____

_____

_____

_____

GOD'S BEST STEWARD

How do His seven sayings from the cross relate to Jesus' stewarding through hardship?

1. When people took from Him He gave _____

   _____ (Luke 23:34)

2. When people who spoke against Him came back for His help, He _____

   _____ (Luke 23:43)

3. When He was unable to take care of His family, He _____

   _____ (John 19:26)

4. When He felt alone, He _____

   _____ (Matthew 27:46)

5. When He had His own needs unfulfilled, He _____

   _____ (John 19:28)

6. When exhausted, He _____

   _____ (John 19:30)

7. When He reached completion of His task, He _____

   _____ (Luke 23:46)

THE SMART STEWARD

Point out a smart aspect of the following stewards

- Noah _____ (Genesis 6:14-16 & 22)

- Joseph _____ (Genesis 41:33-36)

- Bezaleel _____ (Exodus 31:2-4)

- David _____ (1 Samuel 17:38-40)

- Solomon _____ (1 Kings 3:23-27)

12 T'S OF STEWARDSHIP

There are 12 areas that we are to steward, known as the 12 T's. I explain each T in Chapter 3 of the book. Rate yourself on a scale of 1 to 10, with one being extremely poor and 10 being excellent service. After you grade yourself, read the bible verse and write down what it speaks to you.

_____ **Steward over our Time** (Ephesians 5:15-16)

_____

_____

_____ **Steward over our Talents** (1 Peter 4:10)

_____

_____

_____ **Steward over our Treasures** (Matthew 25:21)

_____

_____

_____ **Steward over our Temple** (1 Corinthians 6:19-20)

_____

_____

_____ **Steward over our Thoughts** (2 Corinthians 10:5)

_____

_____

_____

Steward over our Testimony (Revelation 12:11)

_____

_____

Steward over our Treatment (Romans 13:10)

_____

_____

Steward over our Trust (Proverbs 3:5)

_____

_____

Steward over our Theology (1 Thessalonians 5:21)

_____

_____

Steward over our Temper (Ephesians 4:26-27)

_____

_____

Steward over our Thankfulness (1 Thessalonians 5:18)

_____

_____

Steward over our Tongue (Matthew 12:36-37)

_____

_____

_____

NAME IT AND CLAIM IT:

Consider a name for the endeavor for which you wrote a vision statement in section 2. The name is: _____

> *"No Problem of human making is too great to be overcome by human ingenuity, human energy, and the untiring hope of the human spirit."*
> ~ *William J. Clinton:*

NOTES:

_____

_____

_____

_____

_____

_____

_____

_____

_____

_____

_____

_____

_____

_____

_____

_____

_____

FINANCIAL GOALS LIST

Financial Goals	Short Term	Long Term	Priority Goals
1.			
2.			
3.			
4.			
5.			
6.			
7.			
8.			
9.			
10.			
11.			
12.			

EVERY GOOD ENDEAVOR

A SERVANT'S SEASONS

Watch the short video: Be Fruitful

A SERVANT'S SEASONS

SEASSONS

Seasons ae noticeable changes that endure for a span of time that repeat in cycles over time. We endure phaycical seasons based on weather patterns, social seasons based on societal habits and trends and spiritual seasons based on the development of our souls.

For everything there is a season, and a time for every purpose under heaven.
Ecclesiastes 3:1

SPIRITUAL SEASONS

Spiritual seasons derive from six methods of spiritual drawing God uses to bring us near. These **DRAWING (Deliverance, Reward, Active, Wilderness, Inspiration, Need, Growth)** seasons are areas that bring the Spirit-led to service and the flesh-led believer to ruin.

A Season of Deliverance: The season of deliverance contains tests, trials, and spiritual warfare. It is a season of spiritual strengthening, during which the believer's endurance under pressure releases the anointing to conquer sin, temptation, and the devil.

A Season of Reward: The reward season is when God leaves blessings as breadcrumbs to bring you near. This season gives us grateful hearts that endure through every other season we enter.

A Season of Activity: The season of activity is when we labor with the hope of reaping the rewards in due season. Though we are busy, God shows us how not to be in a rush by doing everything with a calm spirit.

A Wilderness Season: This is the dry season in our lives where things don't seem to be going our way. Our struggle is with learning to take the time for self-care and maintaining a spiritual connection.

A Season of Inspiration: This is a season where the **IRIS (Inspiration, Revelation, Insight, Suggestion)** of our mind's understanding opens. God's eyes are upon us, and He supplies inspiration to strengthen and motivate us to enter our season of activity.

A Season of Growth: In the season of growth, God allows us to see the changes in us where our reactions have matured. We come to decisions to follow God more closely and faithfully.

ASSESS

THE SOWER AND THE REAPER

"Behold, the days come," says Yahweh, "that the plowman shall overtake the reaper,
and the one treading grapes him who sows seed; and sweet wine
will drip from the mountains, and flow from the hills."
Amos 9:13

What do the following verses tell you about the Sower and the Reaper

- They should _____ (Genesis 26:12)
- They are _____ (John 4:36)
- They can _____ (John 4:38)
- They _____ (1 Corinthians 3:6)
- They require _____ (2 Corinthians 9:10-11)

What do the following verses say about sowing wrongly:

2 Corinthians 9:6 _____

_____

Proverbs 22:8 _____

_____

Galatians 6:8 _____

_____

Hosea 8:7 _____

_____

Job 4:8 _____

_____

SEASONS IN STEWARDSHIP

The seasons dictate the flow of work of any steward going into business or developing a side hustle for themselves. As businesses grow, you must innovate and refresh your seasonal cycle to stay ahead. There are five cycles, each requiring joint action: plowing & tilling, fertilizing & sowing, weeding & watering, reaping & gathering, and storing & selling.

Plowing and Tilling: Plowing is a process that involves deep breaking up of heavily impacted soil to provide plants with a pathway that improves aeration and irrigation penetration, or provides more access to air and water. Tilling stirs the topsoil, allowing for the removal of weed roots while creating a fine-textured planting zone and a smooth surface for planting. Both require labor and tools to prepare the soil. What heavy and light equipment do you have or need to achieve the goals you listed in section two?

_____

_____

_____

_____

Fertilizing and Sowing: This is where the stinky and dirty work occurs. We must ensure our endeavors are in fertile ground, having a demand that we can supply. Advertising can create a sense of fertility by simplifying someone's task or life. The seeds you are planting are resources you give up to bring an increase. What promotional and financial resources are needed to accomplish the goals mentioned above?

_____

_____

_____

_____

Weeding and Watering: This protects the life of what is about to grow. Weeding is a strategic maneuvering of whatever can cause injury to what you are producing. Watering is a nurturing of what you sown so that it grows healthy. It's about protecting your business, ministry endeavor, or side hustle. What general guidelines, policies, and evaluations will be necessary for you to maintain your endeavor?

_____

_____

_____

Reaping and Gathering: Reaping is removing what has grown from the useless shoots and stalks. Gathering deals with bundling useful products together. These functions require a workforce to complete the efforts. Who are the people you need to accomplish the vision you stated in section two, and what functions do they provide?

_____

_____

_____

_____

Storing and Selling: Storing places resources harvested for future use, while selling earns a profit to provide financial stability. These are equivalent to making money and saving a portion to reinvest into the further development of your endeavor. What are the future needs that you can anticipate that will help your endeavor grow?

_____

_____

_____

_____

IT'S FOR YOU

Combine the vision statement and goals from section 2, the name in section 3, with the answers you placed in the apply portion of section 4, and you have an administrative plan for your business, side hustle, or ministry endeavor. Put it together, pray over it, refine the plan, and put it into action. It is for you, and God is with His steward.

The goal of a simplified administrative plan is that others in your circle, whom you incorporate into the project, should be able to read, understand, and contribute to it immediately. Instead of giving a business example that may divert you from your particular purpose, the following is an example I used in ministry. Note: An exhaustive business plan for investors typically includes demographics, marketing studies, portfolio analysis, a comprehensive vision, history, and functional standards. We reserve this level of detail for large-scale investors. For our personal and family purposes, a brief administrative plan is sufficient.

EXAMPLE
Financial Literacy Seminar Administrative Plan

Purpose: Create a Financial Literacy Educational Platform.

Objectives: Reach out to Crossing members and guests from the local and church community with principles of better money management.

Goal: Enhance the church's knowledge base of financial literacy and foster connections with the community.

Seminar Plan:

- 4-step targeting program for invite includes 1) save the date email, 2) social media notices, 3) 2-week drip campaign, and 4) E-registration

- One-day gathering consisting of 5 financial literacy workshops of 40 minutes apiece

- A follow-up questionnaire to assess whether there is a continual interest and need for continuing courses.

Event Staffing Needs

- Two-person parking and security from 9 am to 10 am

- 2-person registration Saturday 9:00-10:00 am

- Two-person hospitality team Saturday 8:30 – 1:00 pm

- Audio/Visual Team: at least one person scheduled from 8:30 am to 2 pm

- Two-member clean-up crew at 2 pm

Registration materials:

- Sign-in sheet with name, church, and contact information

- Folder containing workshop materials

- A small bottle of water, mints, a pen, and a paper tablet

Agenda:

- 9:00 am – 9:10 am: Greetings, event announcements, and prayer

- 9:10 am – 9:40 am: Basic Financial Principles (How money works)

- 9:40 am – 9:50 am Break

- 9:50 am – 10:30 am: Goals, Careers, and Income (the money you earn)

- 10:35 am – 11:15 am: Savings, Investing, and Retirement Planning (the money you keep)

- 11:20 am – 12:00 pm: Money Management (the money you spend)

- 12:00 pm – 12:15 pm Need for Credit Repair

- 12:15 pm to 1:00 pm No Host Lunch

- 1:00 pm to 1:40 pm Insurance, Wills, Living Trust (the money you protect)

- 1:45 pm to 2:00 pm Closing Remarks

Proposed Cost:

- Free attendance

- Printing and material cost $110

- Church outreach account to cover the guest speaker's cost.

Records:

- Attendance Record and Fellowship Report filing

- Post Seminar Questionnaire for follow-up interest.

NOTES:

GIVING IT AWAY AND GETTING IT BACK

GOOD GIVING

Watch the short video: Giving Releases Getting

GOOD GIVING

TRANSFORMATIVE GIVING BUILDS COMMUNITY

Home economics was a preparatory course designed to teach youth practical skills to improve their future quality of life, including the basics of cooking, sewing, and balancing a checkbook. Schools replaced Home Ec with STEM (Science, Technology, Engineering, and Math), shifting the focus from family life to producing a future workforce. Public education no longer instructs on things that promote personal or community needs, such as financial literacy, but rather on what benefits society, like workforce creation. The backbone of foreign missions is teaching skills that benefit personal and community life. It is also the backbone of community outreach, as we share the gospel while building communities, helping with agriculture, and teaching language and etiquette — essentially, Home Ec expanded.

Meditate on and discuss what the following verses say about Foreign Missions (FM) and Community Outreach (CO). Are they truly modeled after each other?

- **Psalm 27:1** ~ FM building homes and CO building households (Psalm 27:1)

- **Genesis 26:19-22** ~ FM digs wells for clean water, CO cleans trash from communities

- **Matthew 25:26-40** ~ FM starting hospitals, CO doing home and hospital visitations for the sick

- **Isaiah 58:7-8** ~ FM feeding and teaching how to farm, CO providing food outreach centers.

POVERTY: IS IT A MOMENT OR MINDSET

Poverty levels are government measures determining eligibility for assistance. However many grow up under the poverty level may not feel poor. This is because while they are financially tapped their families are together and they lovingly support each other. There are many testimonies of what its like growing up poor but happy.

Financial Income growing up does not control your outcome as an adult. Fulfillment in young lives isn't dependent on finances; it comes from family and loved ones. Poverty is a mindset of powerlessness. It is a learned helplessness that leads individuals to believe there is nothing they can do to improve their situation. Those accepting a poverty mindset stagnate their potential. You can grow up rich with a poor mentality, and you can grow up poor with a rich mentality. Anyone's situation can change if they have the right mindset.

What measures can we take to help people overcome a poverty mindset?

Proverbs 13:20 _____

Psalm 35:10 _____

Isaiah 25:4 _____

2 Corinthians 6:18 _____

Colossians 3:16 _____

GIVING AND GETTING

"But who am I, and what is my people, that we should be able to offer so willingly as this? For all things come from you, and we have given you of your own."

1 Chronicles 29:14

What do the following verses say about Reciprocity:

- Getting it ~ Matthew 7:12

_____

_____

_____

- Giving it ~ Romans 13: 8

_____

_____

_____

- Growing it ~ Luke 6:38

_____

_____

_____

- Grateful for it ~ 2 Thessalonians 2:13

_____

_____

_____

From the book, what are the 4 R's of Giving:

- R _____ (Genesis 28:20-22)
- R _____ (Matthew 25:37-40)
- R _____ (Genesis 22:13-14)
- R _____ (2 Corinthians 9:7)

APPLY

Helping Others

Unscramble the Words

OYCRIPEICRT

VTRPEYO

SENDMTI

AYILMF

INSEOVGER

GNRUEOES

GLNEBSIS

VGNGII

NGGIWRO

WHAT WE CAN DO

Considering the four R's, how can we cultivate redemptive relationships with those struggling with long-term financial insecurity and joyfully help them replace their poverty mindset with one of freedom and liberty?

_____

_____

_____

_____

_____

Before helping others, you must ensure that you are healthy enough to give help yourself, which requires examining your own mindset to ensure that no remnants of a poverty mindset remain. What is the condition of your mindset, and how can you improve it?

_____

_____

_____

_____

To teach others, we must first be students ourselves. What will you do to continue to increase your understanding of financial literacy and to help others understand?

_____

_____

_____

_____

NOTES:

BUDGET FORM

My Income This Month

Paychecks (Salary After Taxes, Benefits, And Fees	$
Other Income (After Taxes), For Example: Child Support	$
Total Monthly Income	$

My Expenses This Month

Mortgage, Rent, Including Renters, And Home Insurance	$
Utilities (Like Electricity And Gas)	$
Internet, Cable, And Phones	$
Other Housing Expenses (Like Property Taxes)	$
Groceries And Household Supplies	$
Meals Out And Other Food Expenses	$
Transportation, Taxis, Tolls, And Parking	$
Gas Expense	$
Car Loan And Insurance	$
Health Insurances And Medicine	$
Child Care, Child Support, And Money Given To Family	$
Giving And Donations	$
Entertainment	$
Personal And Beauty Items And Expenses	$
School Cost	$
Debt Repayment	$
Savings	$
Other Expenses	$

Income: $	Minus	Expenses: $	=	$

THE GOD POCKET KINGDOM

UNDERSTANDING THE TITHE

Watch the short video: Don't Become Bound to Debt

UNDERSTANDING THE TITHE

FROM TRIBES INTO A NATION

Israel began as a growing family living under the family rules, instructed and united them under a covenant with Yahweh their God. They lived as temporary residents until lack became an issue leading to a search for stability. Enduring generational hardship followed God and became a nation.

Tribes become nations when nomadic hunter-gatherers transition from being consumers who take from the environment to being producers who cultivate the environment. Financial security follows the same pathway. Those who hunt and gather enough to survive often experience higher insecurity in their environment. When those same people become producers adding to the environment by planting and nurturing growing **PRODUCTS (Produce, Rewards, Organics, Data, Used, Commodities, Textiles, Safeguards),** they are more secure.

Consumers create a tribal subculture where the social environment meets their needs by exploiting their labor. Producers are the backbone of the economic sustainability that has now stabilized the family. Strong families that can live and work together, have an economic plan that they discuss with each individual, and contribute their portion, are the simplest way to create generational wealth. It doesn't take a lot, but a good family economic plan will help the family for generations.

A TENTH ISN'T ALL IT TAKES

"Woe to you, scribes and Pharisees, hypocrites! For you tithe mint, dill, and cumin,
and have left undone the weightier matters of the law: justice, mercy, and faith.
But you ought to have done these, and not to have left the other undone."
Matthew 23:23

Tithing is only one matter of the law that people struggle with due to failure to understand, faithlessness, or fear. Jesus spoke to the Jewish leaders as if tithing was a foregone conclusion that should not have taken much thought. They were giving a tenth of their spices, which the law did not require them to do. While they thought they were going over and above, Jesus said they weren't doing enough. The law isn't just about our conduct; it's about our character. These are the more challenging and, at times, the more essential things.

What are the Weightier Matters of the Law?

- Micah 6:8 _____

- James 2:13 _____

- Hebrews 11:6 _____

- Mark 12:30-31 _____

- 1 Corinthians 13:13 _____

- Ecclesiastes 12:13 _____

- Romans 12:2 _____

THE FUNCTION OF THE TITHE

The book discusses how, although the word "tithe" means one-tenth, there were three separate tithes taken in Israel. List each one and explain its use and relevance today.

- The Levitical Tithe _____

    _____ (Deuteronomy 10:9)

- The Celebratory Tithe _____

    _____(Deuteronomy 14:23)

- The Mercy Tithe _____

    _____ (Deuteronomy 14:28-29)

THE TRIBUTE TAX

Yahweh said to Samuel, "Listen to the voice of the people in all that they tell you; for they have not rejected you, but they have rejected me as the king over them
1 Samuel 8:7

Israel did not start as a monarchy but a theocracy, meaning God ruled directly. The Lord called the Levites as administrative agents in His government and the heads of families to establish local government supported by a council of elders in towns with their surrounding regions. When Israel asked for a monarch, it was to make their leadership visible, caring more about what other nations or people thought rather than what God had established. Let's review the Levitical functions.

Write one way you can use the Levitical function in your home and family:

1. The Legal System (Deuteronomy 17:9) _____

    _____

2. Worship and Celebrations (1 Chronicles 25:6) _____

_____

3. Educational System (2 Chronicles 17:9) _____

_____

4. Bodyguards (2 Chronicles 23:7) _____

_____

5. Revenue & Welfare System (2 Chronicles 31:14) _____

_____

6. Health and Safety (Leviticus 14:36) _____

_____

7. Transportation (Numbers 1:51) _____

_____

APPLY

What can you do with the three types of Covenants to build your family plan?

- Other-imposed Family Rules (Genesis 6:18)

_____

_____

_____

_____

_____

- Self-Imposed Discipline (Genesis 15:17-18*)

_____

_____

_____

_____

_____

- Mutual Input and Cooperation (Genesis 17:7-8)

_____

_____

_____

_____

_____

Discuss with your family the rules, discipline, and cooperation required in forming a family financial plan, and how each can contribute through coordination, cutting costs, and contributions. If your goal is to buy a house or multiple properties, make sure they understand what it takes. Learn about investing together and assign individuals to research an investment that you can buy into as a family. Even a small investment shows that their input matters, and it helps each to stick to the plan. Use the input above, along with your financial goals list, to create a personalized financial plan tailored to your family's needs.

NOTES:

_____

_____

_____

_____

_____

_____

_____

_____

_____

_____

_____

_____

_____

_____

_____

_____

_____

_____

_____

_____

_____

_____

FAMILY FINANCIAL PLAN

Family Financial Goals: TodaysDate:_____

   1. _____ Achieve By: _____

   2. _____ Achieve By: _____

   3. _____ Achieve By: _____

Family Budget Estimates

   • **We will Spend** $ _____   **We will Save** $ _____

   • **We will Pay Off** $ _____   **We will Invest** $ _____

Anticipated Increase in Budget Needs

Net Worth Total $ _____   **Objective # 2 Cost** $ _____

Objective # 1 Cost $ _____   **Objective # 3 Cost** $ _____

Plan to Cut Spending: _____

_____

_____

_____ **Anticipated Savings $** _____

Ways to Increase Revenue: _____

_____

_____

_____ **Anticipated Increase $** _____

Last Goals Met: Yes_____ No _____   **Reevaluation Date:** _____

THE TREASURE PRINCIPLE

THE SYSTEM OF SACRIFICE

Watch the short video: Three Steps to Success

THE SYSTEM OF SACRIFICE

A SACRIFICIAL WIN

Success requires self sacrifice. Sacrifice is at the heart of every successful team, dream and endeavor, Sacrice not only requires the giving of oncself but the breaking of self so something greater can be seen. Winners believe in themselves because they paid the cost through sacrifice.

Greater love has no one than this, that someone lay down his life for his friends.
John 15:13

Money isn't the measure of greatness, but love and sacrifice. The sacrifices a steward makes to achieve their spiritual, mental, social, and financial goals are a demonstration of love for God and family. In the sacrificial system, everything you offer has a purpose. We can say the same about the personal sacrifices we make to improve our social and financial security, thereby making us safer and more secure. Biblical success is wholeness. We evaluate worldly success by position and possession. The steward never sacrifices their wholeness to gain possessions,

What are the things we cannot sacrifice for success

1. 1 Timothy 5:8 _____

2. Mark 12:30 _____

3. 1 Corinthians 3:17 _____

4. Proverbs 4:23 _____

THE TITHE AND THE SACRIFICES

The book mentions how both tithes and sacrifices collected the same things and brought them to the priest. The Israelites gave both tithes from the flock and grains, and sacrifices from those same flocks and grains. These show us that God accepts the same substances that He shares with us. The difference is that the Israelites set the first tenth apart for use in the Levitical ministry, and anything they gave after that was considered an offering. Tithing is regular giving and sacrifice; it requires that we do more than just the ordinary. Meditate on and discuss the various ways tithing and offerings differ.

Tithes	*Offering*
Used to support the ministry and services	Consumed as a ministry of service
Mandatory giving	Voluntarily given
Based on covenant promises	Repairs breaches in the covenant
An act of faithfulness	An act of worship
Ministers to Need	Ministers to Desire
Collected in the towns	Given at the temple
Maintains our relationship with God	Redeems our relationship with God
Gives the first portion	Gives the best portion
Blessed by the word of God and prayer	Blessed on the altar of God with confession
Given as a tribute of faith	Given as a token of love
Systematic giving	Special occasion giving
Faithful Stewardship	Faith Filled Steward

THE SACRIFICES

For the life of the flesh is in the blood. I have given it to you
on the altar to make atonement for your souls; for it is the
blood that makes atonement by reason of the life.
Leviticus 17:11

The book describes the five bloodied sacrifices and the five unbloodied sacrifices made upon the altar. The priest presented two additional offerings at the altar, but received them back instead of burning them. These bring the number of offerings to twelve, like the number of Jacob's sons, the tribes of Israel, and the apostles. Christian symbolism associates the number 12 with divine order, completeness, and human governance. What relevance does this have to the 12 offerings?

_____

_____

Since life is in the blood, it is the life of the animal that God receives, not its death. What does this speak about the resurrection?

_____

_____

What are the 5 Bloodied Sacrifices?

1. _____ (Leviticus 1:4)

2. _____ (Leviticus 3:1)

3. _____ (Leviticus 4:3)

4. _____ (Leviticus 5:6)

5. _____ (Numbers 19:2-6)

List the 5 Unbloodied Offerings?

6. _____ (Leviticus 2:11)

7. _____ (Numbers 15:5)

8. _____ (Malachi 1:11)

9. _____ (Leviticus 8:28)

10. _____ (Leviticus 2:13)

The unbloodied sacrifices involve rituals, yet two of the unbloodied sacrifices are symbols of the bloody sacrifices that Christ poured out His presence on at the Last Supper. His presence in the elements fulfills the promise made in John chapter 6:53-58. What are these two unbloodied elements, and how are they relevant to the New Testament sacrifices?

_____

_____

_____

_____

What are the remaining 2 Offerings?

11. _____ (Numbers 5:9)

12. _____ (Numbers 18:11)

The last two offerings deal with dedicating things as holy to the Lord. Either they were presented and received back. What significance does this have with dedicating things to God today, whether they be the offering, communion, or our own lives?

_____

_____

_____

REASONS FOR OFFERING

Every man shall give as he is able, according to Yahweh
your God's blessing which he has given you.
Deuteronomy 16:17

We give according to the blessing that God has given to us. The book mentions that every sacrifice has a redemptive purpose. Although some offerings are also based on rituals, those rituals also serve a purpose. When you give an offering, you should connect it with its redemptive purpose and pray that God grants what you are giving for.

Read Chapter 7 In The Book
Match the Offering with its Redemptive Purpose

_____ 1. Burnt   A. Recommitting

_____ 2. Meal   B. Reconciling

_____ 3. Peace   C. Reconnecting

_____ 4. Sin   D. Repairing

_____ 5. Guilt   E. Receiving

_____ 6. Drink   F. Relationship

_____ 7. Red Heifer   G. Restoring

_____ 8. Salt   H. Restitution

_____ 9. Incense   I. Resanctifying

_____ 10. Ordination   J. Obedience

_____ 11. Wave   K. Consecration

_____ 12. Heave   L. Communing

THE STEWARDS' CHARACTER AND SACRIFICE

The sacrificial system addresses our character, calling, and contrition. Each redemptive and ritualistic purpose represents an aspect of ourselves that we must bring before the Lord. For each purpose, list a way you can do this.

1. Repairing Relationships

    _____

    _____

    _____

    _____

2. Reconciling Offense

    _____

    _____

    _____

    _____

3. Restoring the Soul

    _____

    _____

    _____

    _____

4. Restitution to the Offended

    _____

    _____

5. Resanctifying the Self

_____

_____

_____

_____

6. Reconnecting with Others

_____

_____

_____

_____

7. Recommitting to God

_____

_____

_____

_____

8. Relationship Building

_____

_____

_____

_____

9. Consecrating Yourself

_____

_____

_____

_____

10. Staying Obedient

_____

_____

_____

_____

11. Communing with God

_____

_____

_____

_____

12. Receiving from the Lord

_____

_____

_____

_____

NOTES:

_____

_____

_____

_____

_____

_____

_____

_____

_____

_____

_____

_____

_____

_____

_____

_____

_____

_____

_____

_____

_____

REFRESH YOUR RESUME

Write or refresh a one-page resume using the following format

- **Name and Contact Information:** Including name, address, phone number, and email. Do not list social media outlets, but please ensure your social media presence is adequate, as some employers and lenders investigate the social media profiles of individuals and companies they want to hire or associate with.

- **A Summary of Experience:** Summarize your areas of experience, listing the job types you have performed (One sentence) and listing the relevant skills you possess to perform the position you are applying for (One sentence).

- **Areas of Expertise:** List specific areas of expertise you have, such as sales, marketing, Microsoft Office, and auto repair. Also, list languages you are fluent in if bilingual.

- **Skills and Competencies:** List hard (technical) skills and soft (interpersonal) skills that will help you promote yourself. Ensure that you place any licenses or certifications first, as they are often required to fulfill the job qualifications. Be concise, but use technical language whenever possible. Do not use acronyms unless they are specific to the field.

- **Job Experience:** List your work history in reverse chronological order, starting with the most recent position and working backward to the oldest. List the dates when you started and left, with the company's contact information for future reference. Include a list of achievements while employed.

- **Education:** List your education, including the degree level, schools attended, and year graduated. Include any certifications, achievements, and participation in club organizations, along with their corresponding dates.

- **Awards:** List awards, whether they are job-related, charitable, or social organizations.

THE GENEROSITY HABIT

GENEROSITY THAT WORKS

Watch the short video: Blessings

GENEROSITY THAT WORKS

BATTLING MANIPULATIVE GIVING

The thief only comes to steal, kill, and destroy. I came that they
may have life, and may have it abundantly.
John 10:10

Generous giving is a matter of the heart where our love flows from the heart to our hands. However, manipulators depend on the heart. That's why it's essential to know the soil you sow into. I'm not one to say that God never gave someone insight into how to raise funds. He utilized several prophets and leaders to inspire the people to contribute to the construction of the tabernacle and the Second Temple. However, people see an insight God gave for a specific time and repeat it because of its initial effect, turning simple giving into a manipulative tradition where deceit, exploitation, and control are visible. Manipulators not only depend on generosity but also on greed, exchanging promises for payment, and acting as prophets for profit. Offerings already have redemptive power and need no additional promise beyond the blessing of faithfulness.

Jesus warned about the thief. Who are they according to the following verses:

1. John 10:1, John 10:5, and John 10:8 _____

2. Matthew 7:15 _____

3. Jeremiah 23:1 _____

4. Malachi 3:8 _____

WHAT MAKES GIVING GOOD

The things that make giving good are the blessings and the benefits. Emotionally giving is a two-sided coin. Giving not only creates the joy of helping others, but it also avoids later negative emotions that arise after we neglect to help someone and later feel regret. Giving also enhances our social connections, fostering trust, cooperation, and a sense of belonging. People who give are more grateful for what they have, which increases their praise to God and decreases their temptations to sin in pursuit of wealth. Studies show that giving also has increased health benefits.

What do the following verses say about why we give?

1. 1 Corinthians 4:7 _____

   _____

2. 1 Peter 2:9 _____

   _____

3. James 2:5 _____

   _____

4. James 2:16-17 _____

   _____

5. Luke 12:48 _____

   _____

THE FREEDOM OF FREEWILL

saying, "Father, if you are willing, remove this cup from me.
Nevertheless, not my will, but yours, be done.
Luke 22:42

According to the book, the freewill offering is not an offering for redemptive or ritualistic purposes. It is an offering given while rejoicing and always receives the recognition of God. What do the following verses say about the Freewill Offering?

1. 2 Corinthians 8:3-5 _____

2. Ezra 1:5-6 _____

3. Exodus 35:29 _____

4. Leviticus 22:23-24 _____

5. 2 Corinthians 8:12 _____

6. 2 Corinthians 9:7 _____

7. Psalms 54:6 _____

In chapter 7, we learned that in four of the five bloodied offerings, the Israelites could offer a female from the flock. Chapter 8 shows us God accepted deformed animals as a freewill offering. What does this tell us about our need for wisdom and biblical theology?

_____

_____

_____

_____

_____

_____

_____

_____

FIRST FRUITS

Bikkurim (First Fruits) was celebrated with the 7 grains of the land wheat, barley, grapes, figs, pomegranates, olives and dates. Without the temple Jews carry on the spirit of bikkurim basket in the Passover Sedar plate with thanksgiving appreciating the good God gives.

How are FirstFruits given

- They were given _____ (Nehemiah 10:35)

- They were given _____ (Deuteronomy 26:2)

- They were given _____ (Leviticus 23:11)

What are the 3 Blessings of FirstFruits

- Firstfruits _____ (Romans 11:16)

- Firstfruits _____ (Ezekiel 44:30)

- Firstfruits _____ (Proverbs 11:25)

Who are the FirstFruits

- Of the resurrection _____ (1 Corinthians 15:20-21)

- Of God's creation _____ (Deuteronomy 26:2)

- Of salvation _____ (1 Corinthians 16:15)

- Of the Spirit _____ (Romans 8:23)

A CONTINUATION OF FIRSTFRUITS

With no temple or priest to wave the sheaf before the altar, the Jewish people symbolize the first fruits by giving thanks and eating the grains in the Passover Seder plate. The Seder plate is the same plate from which Jesus took bread and made a grain offering, giving thanks to God, which Christians call the Eucharist, meaning thanksgiving or the Communion meal. What does this mean to you?

_____

_____

_____

_____

First fruits taught the Israelites to give the first portion of the harvest to God. They would fast that day until after the Firstfruits were received. The early church would also fast before they received communion. Is there any relevance to this?

_____

_____

_____

_____

Although it brings blessings into people's lives, only a small percentage of churches today practice Firstfruits as a Freewill offering, which is an extra yearly offering that some may not want to bother with. After reading the chapter, what is your opinion of modern-day Firstfruit celebrations?

_____

_____

_____

_____

NOTES:

_____

_____

_____

_____

_____

_____

_____

_____

_____

_____

_____

_____

_____

_____

_____

_____

_____

_____

_____

_____

_____

_____

YOUR PROFESSIONAL PORTFOLIO

If you updated your resume in the last section, it's time to tighten it up and turn it into a professional portfolio. A Professional portfolio isn't just for models. Scientists, teachers, engineers, and those going for competitive jobs use them. Even some business owners include a portfolio in their business plan to secure loans from banks and money market lenders.

- Professional portfolios are bound in booklet form, featuring a color photo of you on the cover that displays your name and the type of business of your specialty.

- A short table of contents, located behind the cover, lists the contents, with each section separated by tabs, allowing interested parties to find essential details easily.

- The First section is your updated resume, followed by previous performance evaluations in the next section. These provide companies with a view of your skills and your level of work and cooperation within the company.

- The following two sections are samples of your work or writing samples, and a list of special projects you led or cooperated on. These provide them with a deeper understanding of the quality of work they can expect from you.

- The subsequent section includes copies of your degrees and educational certifications to expedite any background check and highlight your qualifications during an interview.

- The final section includes certificates of awards, community service records, and letters of recognition. These enhance the sense of a good fit for the company among staff who are well-known in the community.

SPENDING LESS AND LIVING MORE

SAVING AND SPENDING

Watch the short video: Out of Order

SAVING & SPENDING

SAVE FROM WHAT YOU SPEND

Saving money is about saving yourself from spending. Yes, consumers need to be saved from their own spending tendencies. These tendencies are sometimes so automatic we spend before we think. It is our tendencies that get us into financial trouble.

DISCIPLINED SPENDING

There are three principles of saving from what you spend. First, we must watch our bad spending habits. Second, we must cut back on things we can live without. Lastly, we must resist the temptation of dipping into our savings for things we want but don't need.

What do the following verses say about our shopping tendencies

- Luke 12:15 _____
- Luke 12:33-34 _____
- Luke 16:11 _____
- 2 Peter 2:19 _____
- Proverbs 28:19 _____
- Deuteronomy 8:18 _____
- 1 Corinthians 10:13 _____

Financial Literacy Crossword Puzzle

Solve the puzzle using the clues provided below.

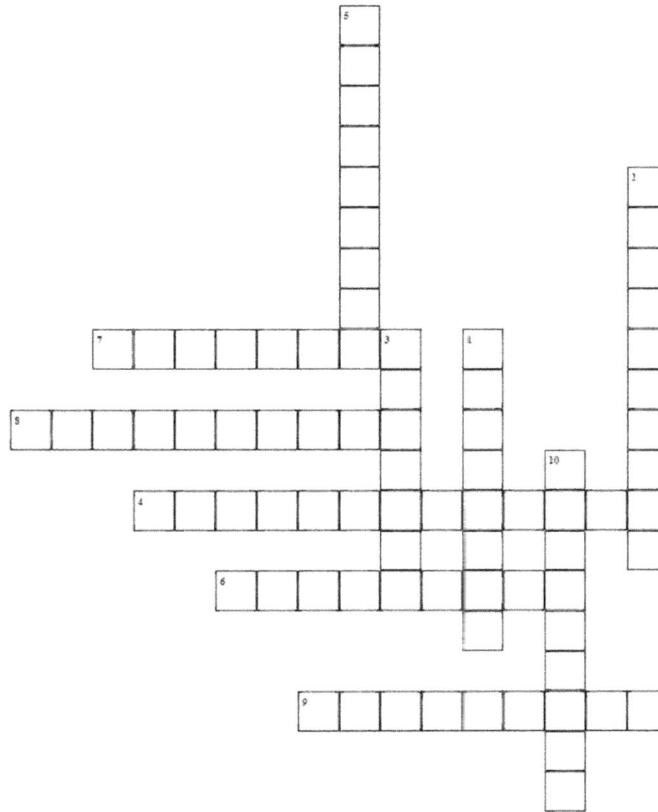

Across

[4] Announcing a product
[6] Paying the highest debt first
[7] End-use purchaser
[8] Spending to get a profit
[9] Loss of purchasing power

Down

[1] A system of money
[2] Being successful
[3] Contribution of after-tax dollars
[5] Earnings after tax
[10] GDP decline

SAVING AND STRATEGY

He who tills his land shall have plenty of bread, but he
who chases fantasies is void of understanding.
Proverbs 12:11

What does the Bible say about Saving

- _____ (Proverbs 13:7)
- _____ (Proverbs 13:22)
- _____ (Proverbs 19:2)
- _____ (Proverbs 21:5)
- _____ (Proverbs 27:23)
- _____ (Proverbs 30:24-26)

What do scriptures say about managing our debt?

- _____ (Proverbs 22:7)
- _____ (Romans 13:8)
- _____ (Psalms 37:21)
- _____ (Romans 13:17)
- _____ (Philippians 4:19)
- _____ (Ecclesiastes 5:4)

The book discusses managing your financial life in a manner similar to how companies operate. Companies establish policies and set goals to ensure efficiency, equity, and expansion, ultimately leading to economic growth. Desiring to be a CEO at work but not handling your personal finances as a CEO isn't wise. Check off each step that you have completed to accomplish this:

Having a Budget _____   Cutting Cost _____

Savings Strategy _____   Strategic Spending _____

Paying Down Debt _____   Invest Strategically _____

Maximizing Income _____   Using Less to Do More _____

APPLY

PRAYER FOR DEBT RELEASE

Heavenly Father, you know my needs. I come confessing that I have not always made the right decisions. I ask you to forgive me for every time I have strayed from your word. As your child, I come to you asking for your help to break the cycle of debt in my life. I cast my burdens on you. I pray that lenders reduce their penalties, interest payments, and debt. I pray for increase, not so I can be rich, but so I can represent you more faithfully. Strengthen and guide me to walk in your ways so that you are magnified, in Jesus' name, Amen.

List 6 Things that you want for your life.

1. _____   4. _____

2. _____   5. _____

3. _____   6. _____

List 6 Things that God wants for your life.

1. _____   4. _____

2. _____   5. _____

3. _____   6. _____

Comparing your wants with God's desire for your life, how closely do you line up?

_____

_____

_____

_____

_____

_____

Reread Genesis 41:15-36. What does it say about:

Times of abundance and lean times _____

_____

Financial Preparations _____

_____

How much Income to live off of _____

_____

Considering your financial situation, what steps can you take to move closer to this plan?

_____

_____

_____

_____

_____

_____

_____

NOTES:

MAKING A SAVINGS PLAN

Knowing how much you want to save isn't tricky, but actually saving that amount takes discipline. Of course, the best way to save is to spend less each month, which means you have to curb your habits. Breaking spending habits takes time and practice, but can be accomplished by anyone. Once you set your mind to do it, you will also need a savings plan.

SAVINGS FINANCIAL GOAL = MONTHLY SAVINGS · NUMBER OF MONTHS

If you wanted to save $9,000 over the next three years, you would calculate that in 36 months, you would have to save $250 a month. If you already know what you can save monthly, then divide that amount by your savings goal, and you will have the number of months it will take to reach your goal. If you have a time limit without a monthly savings goal, divide the number of months by your total savings goal to determine the amount you need to save each month. Either way works. Whatever you want to save, provide a reasonable timeframe for saving it, and put the plan into action. It's a simple formula, but it doesn't account for interest earned.

WITH COMPOUND INTEREST

If your saving financial goal is in an interest-earning account that is compounding each month, the formula is: $FV = P \times (1+r) n-1/n$. (F=Future Value, P=Payment, R=Interest Rate, N=Number of deposits. If your account had earned 5% interest on those same $250 payments for the same 3 years, you would have $9,728.70. If you paid the same amount each month for 10 years, instead of saving $30,000, you would have $38,982.32. That's the power of compound interest. Instead of using a formula, using an online savings calculator can do the work for you.

BUSINESS FOR THE GLORY OF GOD

WORKING FOR GOD'S GLORY

Watch the short video: Knowledge Leads to Success

WORKING FOR GOD'S GLORY

A SERVANT THAT BLESSES GOD

As servants we glorify God in our suffering, but we also glorify Him in our success. Our success is God's success in us and as we achieve greater things He is glorified in our test, triumph and testimonies

Everyone who is called by my name, and whom I have created for my glory,
whom I have formed, yes, whom I have made.
Isaiah 43:7

There is no doubt that God created us for His glory. Whether good or bad, we have opportunities to give God glory. Some say success is the best revenge, but it's actually the best way to show God's glory. Every biblical character who submits to God, He makes into a success story. We should believe that God wants us to be successful in both our spiritual walk and our lives. Pick one of the following stories, meditate on it, and discuss the following with someone.

David, from the forgotten shepherd to a King

Joseph from slave to Egypt's Prime Minister

Daniel from captivity to Chief Governor

Elisha from servant to Prophet of Israel

Paul from persecutor to prisoner for Christ

Peter, from a rude fisherman to an Apostle

John from Son of Thunder to Apostle of Love

Timothy, from a shy youth to a Strong Leader

List ways we can bring glory and praise to God:

1. Psalms 63:3 _____

2. Malachi 2:2 _____

3. Matthew 5:16 _____

4. John 14:13 _____

5. 1 Corinthians 6:20 _____

6. 1 Corinthians 10:31 _____

7. 2 Corinthians 9:13 _____

8. Philippians 1:20 _____

9. 1 Peter 2:12 _____

10. 1 Peter 4:16 _____

With all these ways to give God glory in mind, what way are you using in your life?

_____

_____

_____

_____

2 Samuel 22:21 says God rewards us according to our cleanliness and righteousness. Have you positioned yourself for His reward? What can you do now to make it so?

_____

_____

_____

_____

Describe the Pareto Principle in your own words and how you can use it to help succeed.

_____

_____

_____

_____

_____

TIME TO MEET OUR GOALS

Revisiting Chapter Two of the book, it states that daily goals form habits, short-term goals allow us to track progress, and long-term goals represent our vision. Explain your goals.

- My daily goals are: _____

_____

_____

_____

- My short-term goals are: _____

_____

_____

_____

- My long-term goal is: _____

_____

_____

_____

PROGRESSING FORWARD

Commit your deeds to Yahweh, and your plans shall succeed.
Proverbs 16:3

Someone once said that the biggest room in any home is the room for improvement. Wherever you are in your financial stewardship journey, there is always a higher place for you to go: more to learn and better ways to innovate by incorporating new knowledge and technology into our endeavors. What areas of financial stewardship do you need to learn more about, and how can you acquire this knowledge?

_____

_____

_____

_____

Who in your life can you learn this from?

_____

_____

_____

_____

Eventually, we hope to retire and enjoy the fruits of our years of hard work and good stewardship. However, many continue to work either because they still have financial needs or because they need a sense of purpose. How prepared are you both mentally and financially for retirement?

_____

_____

_____

_____

List Four Principles about Investing

1. _____ (Proverbs 21:5)

2. _____ (Proverbs 24:3-4)

3. _____ (Job 6:11)

4. _____ (Ecclesiastes 11:2)

REPAIRING YOUR CREDIT

The book emphasizes the importance of relying only on what has proven itself faithful. As stewards, we order our steps according to what is dependable. Our credit score is a measure of our financial trustworthiness. Using your bank or a free credit app, what is your credit score, and what do you need it to be?   **Score** _____   **Minimum Desired Score** _____

If your credit needs repair, what methods are you using to improve it?

Avalanche _____   Automating Bills _____

Snow Balling _____   Boost Services _____

Piggybacking _____   Credit Builder Apps _____

Disputing Discrepancies _____   Payoff Agreements _____

What do the scriptures say about collateral and co-signing:

• Proverbs 17:18 _____

• Proverbs 27:13 _____

• Proverbs 22:26-27 _____

NOTES:

_____

_____

_____

_____

_____

_____

_____

_____

_____

_____

_____

_____

_____

_____

_____

_____

_____

_____

_____

_____

_____

_____

_____

CREATE AN INVESTMENT STRATEGY

Those new to investing should consider consulting a financial advisor. Make them your partner for your financial planning. We need to learn so that we gain a thorough understanding of the concepts they are attempting to explain to us. It is advisable to have an emergency fund in place and control your debt when starting to invest. If the interest you pay on debt is greater than the interest you earn from investing, you won't gain any earnings.

- We are to invest from our disposable income. We will be holding up our personal usage of this money for some time so that it can serve as a seed and grow. Your budget should determine what you can invest in and how often.

- Your long-term and short-term financial goals will define your investment timeline. Sometimes we have ideas for money that we don't need now but will need in a year or so. In such cases, a secure investment is the best option.

- Your risk tolerance is essential. The greater the risk, the higher the potential gains, so undervalued stocks could be beneficial; however, someone undervalues them for a reason. Investing is a potentially high-stakes endeavor for those undertaking it without knowledge. It becomes a well-informed decision for those possessing both knowledge and experience.

- Decide where to invest and periodically check on it. As stewards of God, we are not to invest in things that contradict our principles. Find the right fit, and check on it periodically. Gains and losses occur regularly. Don't panic. Learn more before making moves.

CONCLUSION

That the blessing of Abraham might come on the Gentiles through Christ Jesus,
that we might receive the promise of the Spirit through faith.

Galatians 3:14

We pray that God will use you extensively as a servant and steward of His kingdom, and that God will bless your life as a result. Stewardship God's way requires our right attitude and faithfulness. I applaud you for your journey and encourage you to keep learning and moving forward. The book and guide were not just to inform but also to help you. Upon completing this guide, you will have several tools at your disposal. Including:

- A Calculation Of Your Net Worth

- A Prepared Budget

- An Administrative Plan For A Business Or Ministry

- A List Of Your Financial Goals

- A Family Financial Plan

- A Professional Portfolio Alongside A New Resume

- A Savings Plan

- An Investment Strategy

Use these to further your journey as God's Steward, allowing Him to bless your life with the abundance of His peace and grace.

PUZZLE ANSWERS

B	I	P	M	A	N	A	G	E	R	H	O	E	Y	X	J	V	K
D	G	I	O	W	N	E	R	S	W	D	C	T	R	K	B	D	X
N	H	H	S	B	Z	N	I	X	B	N	I	Z	D	C	O	S	Q
I	B	S	L	O	P	C	T	K	E	L	R	F	L	O	L	K	X
F	L	D	O	C	I	T	N	U	I	K	D	W	I	W	G	E	J
F	E	R	Y	I	Q	I	L	B	S	E	X	E	W	E	P	N	T
Q	I	A	A	Q	N	F	A	I	G	E	N	E	R	O	U	S	K
G	W	W	L	C	N	T	O	O	L	C	K	J	G	R	V	T	F
U	X	E	B	I	N	G	B	M	M	A	G	L	V	O	G	Z	C
W	E	T	Y	U	C	E	N	R	L	R	O	R	G	N	O	A	P
F	O	S	O	I	S	H	Y	N	E	W	E	N	I	A	Z	A	G
N	B	C	E	E	B	L	F	E	Q	T	Q	D	T	N	R	V	Z
F	C	D	P	J	R	V	D	P	S	R	R	W	B	T	X	J	H
A	Z	A	B	V	O	V	L	A	F	A	I	T	H	F	U	L	C
F	I	T	M	M	O	H	M	Q	O	O	C	K	B	R	L	S	A
X	J	M	X	D	H	H	U	R	B	X	F	T	F	R	C	W	
P	U	V	S	N	L	P	U	B	P	Z	L	Y	O	C	M	L	H
G	N	M	T	B	S	Y	J	K	E	Q	O	R	G	R	S	V	P

Word Scramble Answer

OYCRIPEICRT	R E C I P R O C I T Y
VTRPEYO	P O V E R T Y
SENDMTI	M I N D S E T
AYILMF	F A M I L Y
INSEOVGER	S O V E R E I G N
GNRUEOES	G E N E R O U S
GLNEBSIS	B L E S S I N G
VGNGII	G I V I N G
NGGIWRO	G R O W I N G

Matching Words Answer

D	1. Burnt	A.	Recommitting
C	2. Meal	B.	Reconciling
B	3. Peace	C.	Reconnecting
G	4. Sin	D.	Repairing
H	5. Guilt	E.	Receiving
A	6. Drink	F.	Relationship
I	7. Red Heifer	G.	Restoring
J	8. Salt	H.	Restitution
F	9. Incense	I.	Resanctifying
K	10. Ordination	J.	Obedience
L	11. Wave	K.	Consecration
E	12. Heave	L.	Communing

CrosswordPuzzleAnswer

```
                    ⁵N
                     E
                     T
                     I
                     N
                     C
                     O                              ²P
                     M                               R
    ⁷C O N S U M E ³R                                O
                     O          ¹C                   S
    ⁸I N V E S T M E N T         U                   P
                     H          R                    E
                                R        ¹⁰R          R
      ⁴A D V E R T I S E M E N T        C            I
                     R          N        E           T
        ⁶A V A L A N C H E       Y       S           Y
                                 Y       S
                    ⁹I N F L A T I O N
                                         O
                                         N
```

www.ingramcontent.com/pod-product-compliance
Lightning Source LLC
Chambersburg PA
CBHW081745200326
41597CB00024B/4394

9 781965 441077